DECOUPAGE
Simple and Sophisticated

LITTLE
CRAFT BOOK
SERIES

By
Joan B.
Priolo

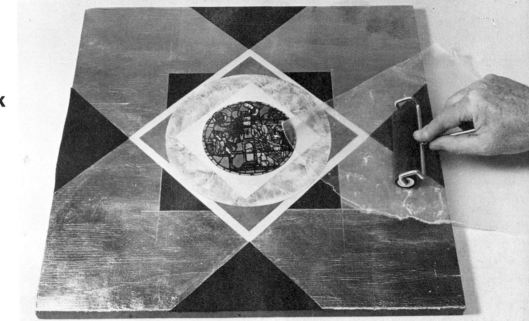

STERLING PUBLISHING CO., INC. NEW YORK

Oak Tree Press Co., Ltd. London & Sydney

SAUNDERS OF TORONTO, Ltd., Don Mills, Canada

Little Craft Book Series

Aluminum and Copper Tooling
Appliqué and Reverse Appliqué
Balsa Wood Modelling
Bargello Stitchery
Beads Plus Macramé
Beauty Recipes from Natural Foods
Big-Knot Macramé
Candle-Making
Cellophane Creations
Ceramics by Slab
Coloring Papers
Corn-Husk Crafts
Corrugated Carton Crafting
Costumes from Crepe Paper
Crafting with Nature's Materials
Creating Silver Jewelry with Beads
Creating with Beads
Creating with Burlap
Creating with Flexible Foam
Creative Lace-Making with Thread and Yarn
Cross Stitchery
Curling, Coiling and Quilling
Decoupage—Simple and Sophisticated

Embossing of Metal (Repoussage)
Enamel without Heat
Felt Crafting
Finger Weaving: Indian Braiding
Flower Pressing
Folding Table Napkins
Greeting Cards You Can Make
Hooked and Knotted Rugs
Horseshoe-Nail Crafting
How to Add Designer Touches to Your Wardrobe
Ideas for Collage
Junk Sculpture
Lacquer and Crackle
Leathercrafting
Macramé
Make Your Own Elegant Jewelry
Make Your Own Rings and Other Things
Making Paper Flowers
Making Picture Frames
Making Shell Flowers
Masks
Metal and Wire Sculpture

Model Boat Building
Monster Masks
Mosaics with Natural Stones
Nail Sculpture
Needlepoint Simplified
Off-Loom Weaving
Organic Jewelry You Can Make
Patchwork and Other Quilting
Pictures without a Camera
Potato Printing
Puppet-Making
Repoussage
Scissorscraft
Scrimshaw
Sculpturing with Wax
Sewing without a Pattern
Starting with Stained Glass
Stone Grinding and Polishing
String Things You Can Create
Tissue Paper Creations
Tole Painting
Trapunto: Decorative Quilting
Whittling and Wood Carving

The author and publishers would like to thank Wayne McCall of Santa Barbara, California, who did the photography for this book.

All of the decoupage objects illustrated were made by the author.

Copyright © 1974 by Sterling Publishing Co., Inc.
419 Park Avenue South, New York, N.Y. 10016
Distributed in Canada by Saunders of Toronto, Ltd., Don Mills, Ontario
British edition published by Oak Tree Press Co., Ltd., Nassau, Bahamas
Distributed in Australia and New Zealand by Oak Tree Press Co., Ltd.,
P.O. Box J34, Brickfield Hill, Sydney 2000, N.S.W.
Distributed in the United Kingdom and elsewhere in the British Commonwealth
by Ward Lock Ltd., 116 Baker Street, London W 1
Manufactured in the United States of America   *All rights reserved*
Library of Congress Catalog Card No.: 73-93597
I I Sterling ISBN 0-8069-5300-4 Trade   Oak Tree 7061-2486-3
5301-2 Library

Contents

NOTE: In this book, trade names have been used in certain projects when particular manufacturers' products only were used and are the only products the author recommends for the kind of work done in those projects. In the photos where trade names appear, it is for the purpose of identifying the type of materials to be used, to aid selection from several suitable manufacturers' products.

Illus. 1

Before You Begin

The art of decoupage is centuries old. It became popular in 18th-century Italy and France as an inexpensive way to simulate the fine, hand-painted furniture of the wealthy. By using paper cutouts, the effects of beautiful, hand-painted scenes and decorations were achieved at low cost.

Decoupage pieces became so beautiful in themselves that, since the 18th century, the craft has had many revivals of popularity. Now, with this book, *you* will be able to participate in a 20th-century revival of decoupage. Because there

have been so many technical advances in the fields of paints, varnishes, and decorative papers, decoupage is an even more exciting art form today than it ever was.

Traditionally, the idea of decoupage is to cover decorative paper cutouts with enough layers of varnish so that, with several sandings, the design eventually sinks into the layers of varnish and becomes level. Because this makes paper edges "recede" so that they cannot be felt, or seen, the illusion of a hand-painted decoration is created.

Since decoupage is a decorative art form, we will try to suggest to you as many ideas for decoration as possible for you to use as a springboard to your own creativity.

For your decoupage projects, use boxes, furniture, glass jars, waste-paper baskets, trays—anything that stands still and has at least one flat surface. For your decorative papers, use gift-wrap paper, magazines, books, wallpaper and notepaper. Save that special greeting card from a special friend and make a special box with it. Keep a vacation memory or dream alive by using cutouts from a travel brochure on a project.

In this book, you will learn how to make use of the decorative papers all around you and also how to make your *own papers* so that you can create decoupage pieces of originality and lasting beauty.

When you have chosen the object you wish to decoupage, remember that some objects, such as boxes, have sides to be considered in the over-all design. Try many combinations. Cut out small individual designs, or try a border design to encircle a bowl or vase or to wrap round a box. Use an entire flower print, or one large, cut motif with small fillers. Cut out small squares of colored paper for a "mosaic" effect.

When you and your object are ready to begin, the basic materials you will need are decorative papers, white glue, a small pair of scissors, clear acrylic spray, a sponge, and some imagination!

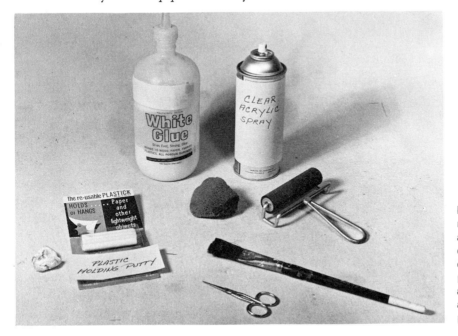

Illus. 2. The basic materials needed to apply your decoupage design are white glue, clear acrylic spray, plastic holding putty, a sponge, a small roller, a brush and a small pair of scissors.

Decoupage a Box with a Greeting Card

Illus. 3. To decoupage a small box, choose the face of a Christmas card and small (1-inch) construction-paper squares.

There is no end to the variety of objects that you can use for decoupage. Choose from chairs, mirror frames, boxes, table tops—just about any object with a flat or smooth surface. If this is your first attempt at decoupage, you might begin with something small and simple, such as a wooden box.

The small box shown in Illus. 3 is about to be decorated with a Christmas card and small construction-paper "mosaic" squares. This box has been painted with three coats of acrylic paint and "antiqued" with paste gold in preparation for its new look.

When you plan to paint a raw wood object, first fill in any holes or defects with gesso or a wood filler. Then, sand the entire surface with #200 garnet sandpaper (coarse), and wipe with a rag or tackcloth. Tackcloth is a waxy cheesecloth.

After your object has been painted, you may want to "antique" it. One of the easiest and most effective methods is with a paste gold (available at art supply shops, or hobby and hardware suppliers). You simply rub it on the painted surface

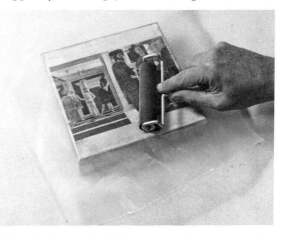

Illus. 4. Paste the Christmas card cutout on the top of the box, and "iron" out the excess glue and air bubbles with a roller over waxed paper.

6

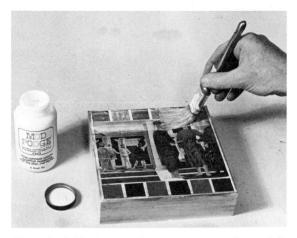

Illus. 5. Add the small squares as a "mosaic" border for the card, and varnish the box with a water-based acrylic varnish, such as Mod Podge.

with your finger or a rag. Rub the gold *lightly* over the surface, going with the grain of the wood. If you overdo it, wipe off the excess with turpentine. Paste gold is excellent also for gilding edges and rims, since you can achieve a solid gold covering if you apply it heavily enough. The light-colored construction-paper squares shown in Illus. 3 were crumpled and rubbed lightly with paste gold.

The next step is pasting. The best all-purpose glue for decoupage is white glue, available under various trade names (Sobo, Elmer's Glue-All, Duratite, and so on). Dilute the white glue with water, generally in the proportion of 3 parts glue

Illus. 6. Paste the greeting on the inside of the card on the inside of the lid. Gift-paper cut-outs decorate the inside of the bottom of the box. See the finished box in color in Illus. 21 and 22.

to 1 part water. You may need to use a thinner mixture for very thin papers and a thicker mixture for heavier papers. Apply the glue to the paper with your fingers or with a brush. If the glue beads, your mixture is too thin. Add more glue.

When pasting large or stiff pieces of paper, you may want to apply glue to the surface of the object as well as to the paper to achieve a firmer hold. Press the paper in place with your fingers, making sure to press out all air bubbles and excess glue. It is often a good idea to place a sheet of waxed paper over the design and roll a small printing roller lightly over the glued area to make doubly sure all air is pressed out. After the paper has set for a few moments, wipe off any excess glue with a wet sponge.

Although a multitude of varnishes is available for decoupage (as you will find out on page 23), you need only use a water-based acrylic varnish (such as Mod Podge) to finish off your first effort.

Illus. 7. Good sources for your design materials include gift-wrap paper, notepaper, prints and books.

Sources of Design Materials

Since decoupage is, after all, a decorative art form, one of your main concerns will be with design. How to decorate the object you have selected? Where to find the decorative papers? Relax. You are probably stumbling over design sources every day! That pile of magazines, those old books in the garage, last season's flower and seed catalogue—all contain design elements.

One of the best and most readily available sources is gift-wrap paper—new or used. Modern gift papers provide a wealth of design, from floral to geometric patterns. Decorative note and letter paper and wallpaper are also good sources.

Try to choose from materials easily accessible to you, especially when starting out. As you progress with decoupage, you may run across more esoteric sources, such as old engravings, reproductions of tapestries and paintings, and so on, but if you start out with these in mind exclusively, you may never get started. Just keep your eyes and mind open, think "decoupage" on your travels, and pick up any likely papers you may see. Even if you don't know what to do with them at the moment, you will eventually find a use for them. At the very worst, you could use gift-wrap paper or notepaper for their intended purposes.

In any case, keep a stockpile of papers as your security blanket against any momentary lack of inspiration. Remember, too, you don't have to rely entirely on printed papers. You can make many beautiful papers of your own as you will find out in the projects that follow.

Decoupage with Acrylics

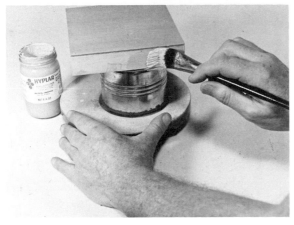

Illus. 8. First paint the box with two or three coats of acrylic paint.

Acrylics can be used from start to finish in a decoupage project. You may want to try acrylics, especially if children are involved in the project, because the brush-on acrylics are water-based, dry in a short time, and are non-toxic and non-flammable.

When you use acrylic paints, you will not have to seal the wood first since acrylic is in itself a sealer. Most of the brush-on paints found in hobby and art supply shops for decoupage purposes are water-based, but check the labels to be sure. With all paints, whether acrylics or not, two or three coats should be sufficient to cover the surface evenly.

Now try decoupaging another box, using acrylics throughout, and this time line it with fabric as shown in Illus. 11 through Illus. 14.

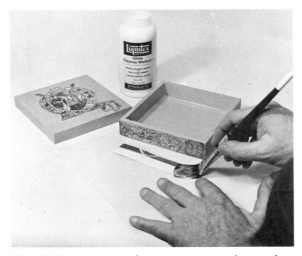

Illus. 9. Paste cutouts from an art magazine on the top and sides of the box with a water-based acrylic emulsion, such as Liquitex Polymer Medium, which can be used both as an adhesive and a varnish.

Illus. 10. Then varnish the box with the polymer medium. Apply as many coats as needed to "sink" the print.

9

Illus. 11. Cut a piece of cardboard the size of the inside dimensions of the bottom of the box. Place the cardboard on the reverse side of the fabric and cut around the cardboard, leaving a $\frac{1}{4}$-inch edge of fabric.

Illus. 12. Snip off the corners of the fabric diagonally.

Lining with Fabric

Illus. 13. Apply full-strength white glue to the edges of the fabric and the cardboard. Turn the edges and paste firmly to the cardboard.

Illus. 14. Turn the fabric-covered cardboard over and place inside the box. See the finished box in color in Illus. 23.

A Small Chest of Drawers

Illus. 15. Paint the chest and the drawers separately with flat black paint and let dry. Placing your objects on a tall tin can makes painting easier.

A helpful aid in the planning stage of a decoration is a plastic holding putty (Illus. 2), available at art and hardware supply shops. Peel off a small piece of the putty, roll it into a ball, and use it to hold your paper cutouts temporarily to any surface. The putty is especially handy for sticking paper cutouts to upright surfaces, such as on this little six-drawer chest. See the completed chest in color on page 29.

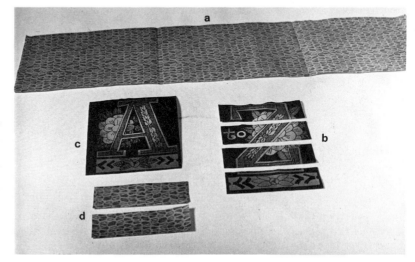

Illus. 16. Cut one piece of wallpaper to go round the two sides and top of the chest (a). Cut four pieces of gift paper for four of the drawers (b) and one piece for the top of the chest (c). Cutouts for the top and bottom drawers of this chest are from the wallpaper (d).

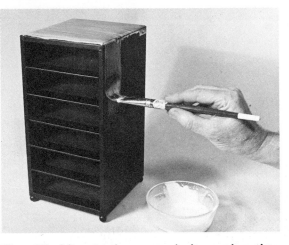

Illus. 17. After testing your design, using the plastic holding putty, apply white glue to the top and sides of the chest and to the long "a" piece.

Illus. 18. Paste the long wallpaper piece (a) round the sides and the top, carefully smoothing small sections at a time.

Illus. 19. Apply white glue to the drawers, and paste the gift paper and wallpaper cutouts ("b" and "d" pieces) on the face of each drawer and the "c" piece on top of the chest.

Illus. 20. Several coats of clear acrylic spray serve as a varnish. The traditional varnishing process (page 23) is unnecessary because there are no raised edges here to "sink."

Illus. 21. A treasured Christmas card transforms a box into a cherished object. Small "mosaics" of black and red construction paper are added for design and interest. (See page 6.)

Illus. 22. The personal greeting section of the Christmas card is used, along with gift-paper cutouts, to line the box in Illus. 21.

Illus. 23. Orange acrylic paint and cutouts from an art magazine create a bright little jewel of a box. (See page 9.)

Illus. 24. Paint two coats of gesso on the jar.

Illus. 25. Rub on paste gold gently.

Illus. 26. Finish with two or three coats of clear acrylic spray.

Decoupage a Glass Jar

In order to prepare either ceramics or glass for decoupaging, clean the surface with soap and water, and then with denatured alcohol. Spray two light coats of clear acrylic spray over the surface as a base for glueing or painting.

First, paint two coats of gesso on the jar. While the second coat is still wet, texture the gesso with the edge of your paintbrush as shown in Illus. 24.

When the textured gesso coat has dried, rub paste gold (page 6) gently over the surface and on the rim of the jar (Illus. 25).

The simple design in Illus. 26 is composed of a border strip and small leaf shapes, all cut out from patterned paper. Paste your design on the jar and then spray the finished jar with two or three coats of clear acrylic spray. Be sure to choose a jar with an attractive shape.

Turn to Illus. 29 to see this jar in color.

14

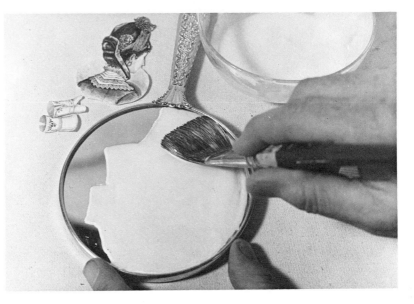

Illus. 27. Choose a two-sided hand mirror with a design appropriate to your cutouts. Paint the magnifying side of the mirror with full-strength white glue.

A Hand Mirror with a "Moonstone" Finish

Illus. 28. Carefully place the gift-wrap-paper cutouts in place on the wet glue and let dry. An old-fashioned design is here used which is complemented by the ornate handle of the mirror. Then...

(Continued on page 18)

Illus. 29. Gesso that you texture yourself serves as an interesting background for the paper cutouts on this glass jar. (See page 14.)

Illus. 30. Gold leaf is the background for this mirror frame. Small cutouts from tapestry illustrations add a subtle decoration to the corners of the frame. See page 42 for applying gold leaf.

Illus. 31. Layers of white glue provide a mysterious "moonstone" background for gift-wrap-paper cutouts on one side of a two-sided hand mirror. (See page 15.)

Illus. 32. A glass bottle is transformed into a striking vase by the use of white gesso and cutouts from a book of plant pictures.

(Continued from page 15)

... cover the face of the mirror with six coats of white glue (Illus. 33). Do not dilute the glue or worry about any unevenness of application. A ripply look adds to the "moonstone" effect of diffused light. Illus. 34 (right). Next, rub diluted black acrylic paint on the mirror handle for a soft antique finish.

Illus. 35. Finally, spray the finished mirror, including the handle, with three coats of clear acrylic spray. See this mirror in color on page 17.

Decoupage
a Metal Tray

Illus. 36. After applying a coat of metal primer, paste a circle of patterned gift-wrap paper on the surface of the tray.

To prepare metal objects for decoupage, clean the surface thoroughly free of oils by using denatured alcohol. Then, apply a coat of metal primer to prevent rusting and as a base for paint-ing. The tray here will have a "paper-doll"-type cutout pasted in the middle. See Illus. 39 on the next page to see the effect of the finished tray in full color.

Illus. 37. Then paint a smaller circle of a solid color with acrylic tube paint and paste it on the gift-wrap paper. This circle is blue.

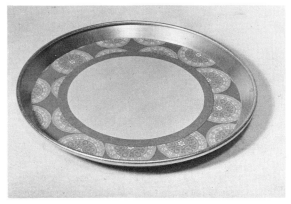

Illus. 38. Cut out a circle of a light-colored construction paper (in this case, yellow) and paste it inside the other circle. Now you are ready to make a "paper-doll" cutout.

Illus. 39. A large, round, metal tray is here decorated with gift-wrap paper, hand-colored paper, construction paper, and a "paper-doll" type of cutout. (See pages 19 and 22.)

Illus. 40. A large, simple cutout and a border are the components for decoupaging a small metal wastebasket.

Illus. 41. This wooden box, painted red, rubbed with paste gold, and decorated with cutouts from gift-wrap paper, has been subjected to 15 coats of varnish! For traditional varnishing, see page 23.

Illus. 42. Large pieces of gift-wrap paper line the box in Illus. 41. To make this box, see page 24.

Illus. 43. A wooden tissue box is painted white, "antiqued" with paste gold and decorated with patterned wallpaper and individual motifs from gift-wrap paper.

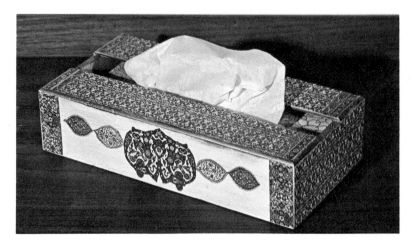

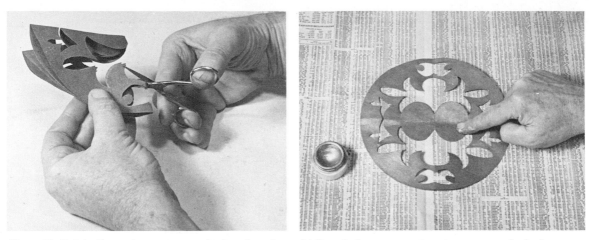

Illus. 44 (left). To make a repeat design for the middle of the tray, cut out a paper circle in a co-ordinating color. Fold the circle twice, and cut out a random pattern. This is the same principle as for cutting out paper dolls. Try a few newspaper cutouts first to get an idea of the results when unfolded. Illus. 45 (right). Unfold the circle and rub the paper lightly with paste gold.

Illus. 46. Paste the "paper-doll" circle over the yellow circle and varnish the tray. Since a tray is subject to spills of all kinds, a polyurethane spray was the varnish used here, because it is impervious to almost anything.

Varnishing

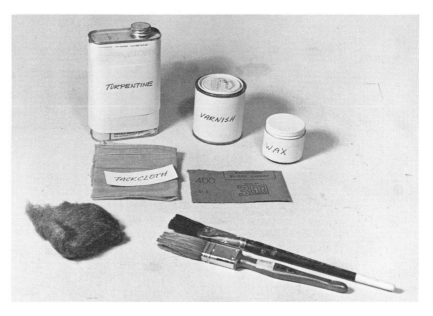

Illus. 47. For the varnishing part of your decoupage projects, you will need varnish, turpentine, varnish brushes, tackcloth, sandpaper, steel wool, and finishing wax.

So many types of varnishes are available under various trade names, that it is impossible to keep track of them all. There are brush-on varnishes, spray varnishes, acrylic varnishes (both spray and brush-on), glossy varnishes and satin (semi-gloss) varnishes. Art supply and hobby shops carry special decoupage varnishes. The water-based varnishes are easy to apply, dry in a matter of minutes, and are softer and, therefore, easier to sand. Some of these water-based varnishes can also be used as an adhesive, as you have already discovered. However, for real permanence, most of these varnishes do require a final coat of a turpentine-based varnish.

As a project, take a box like the one in Illus. 48 through Illus. 59, decorate it with gift-wrap-paper cutouts and paste gold, and subject it to 15 coats of varnish. Before you start the traditional varnishing process in this project, you need a word about just what you are trying to accomplish with all the varnishing and sanding. Basically, you are "sinking" the paper design into layers of varnish so that it becomes as level as a painting. Achieving this "painted" effect usually requires as many as 15 to 20 coats of varnish with a sanding every five or six coats.

This is the traditional method, but with some of the newer varnishes you may get away with fewer coats. Also, in some cases, it is not objectionable to have paper edges *look* like paper edges, so that only two or three coats (preferably a satin varnish) are necessary as a protective coating.

The following is a general procedure for traditional decoupage varnishing:

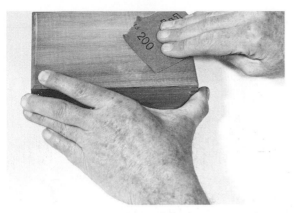

Illus. 48. Choose a raw wood box for this project, and sand the raw wood surface with #200 garnet sandpaper.

Illus. 49. Clear the surface of all sanding dust, and brush on two coats of shellac to seal the raw wood.

Illus. 50. Spray the inside and the outside of the box with a spray enamel. (In this case, red was used.)

Illus. 51. When the paint is dry, rub paste gold lightly over the painted surface to add interest and to soften a bright color.

Illus. 52. Cut out flowers and leaves, or whatever other design pleases you, from gift-wrap paper with a small scissors.

(either before or after cutting) with two light coats of acrylic spray. This will prevent any bleeding of colors from the ensuing layers of varnish. It will also stiffen delicate papers so that they don't shred or tear while you paste them in place.

Now, decide on the type of paint you are going to use, remembering that oil-based paints and enamels, whether spray or brush-on, require the wood to be sealed first with two coats of shellac or clear acrylic spray.

If the surface is raw wood with a clear, beautiful grain, you may not want to paint it a color. In that case, first sand the surface with #200 garnet sandpaper. Wipe off any loose grains with a soft rag or tackcloth after sanding. Then you will have to seal the raw wood surface so that it will take subsequent coats of varnish evenly. The traditional way to seal raw wood is with two

1. Apply six coats of a glossy varnish (check the label for drying time).

2. Sand with #400 wet or dry sandpaper dipped in water.

3. Wipe off all dust particles with a soft rag or tackcloth.

4. Apply five to eight more coats of glossy varnish.

5. Sand with #400 wet or dry sandpaper.

6. Wipe with a rag or tackcloth.

7. Apply two coats of a satin or mat varnish.

8. Gently steel-wool the surface with #0000 steel wool, or rub the surface with pumice powder and linseed oil. (See page 40.)

9. Apply a decoupage finishing wax.

When you have decided on your design, it is a good idea to seal the papers you are going to use

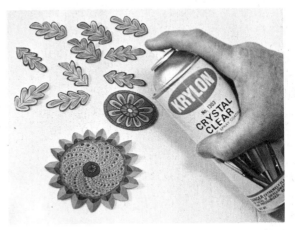

Illus. 53. Spray the cutouts with clear acrylic spray so that the paper colors will not bleed under subsequent coats of varnish.

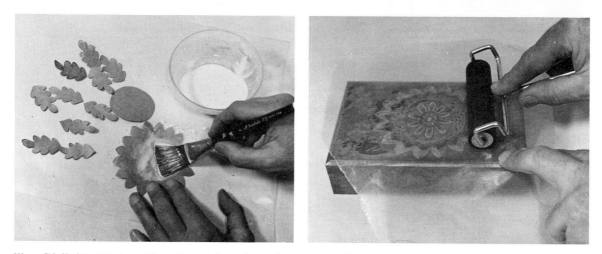

Illus. 54 (left). Dilute white glue and apply to the cutouts. Then press the cutouts firmly in place with your fingers. Illus. 55 (right). Now, place a piece of waxed paper over the design and roll a small roller over the surface to make sure there are no air bubbles.

Illus. 56. Wipe off any excess glue with a wet sponge.

Illus. 57. Cut with a razor blade to separate the design where it has been pasted over the joining of the lid and the bottom of the box.

coats of shellac. However, clear acrylic spray works just as well, is easier to use, and dries faster—in a matter of minutes! If you want to stain the wood, stain it *before* you seal it, or the stain will not sink in.

Make sure that your design is firmly glued in place before you varnish. Check the edges of your cutouts with your fingernail. Edges have a sneaky way of unglueing themselves if you are not on the alert.

Illus. 58. While individual motifs were used on the outside of this box, larger sections of the same gift-wrap paper were used to line the inside of the box. See Illus. 41 and 42 to see the finished box in color.

Illus. 59. Brush glossy varnish on the box and complete the varnishing process as described on page 25. A total of 15 coats of varnish was used on the outside of the box. Only two coats were used on the inside.

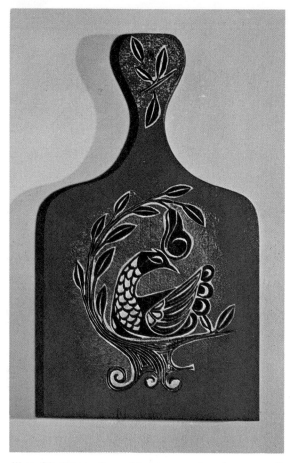

Illus. 60. A breadboard becomes a handsome wall decoration when painted red and decoupaged with notepaper cutouts. (See page 30.)

Illus. 61. Small squares of colored paper, rubbed with paste gold, alternate with strips of gift-wrap paper to create this handsome pencil holder for your desk.

Illus. 62. To decoupage on plastic, no special treatment is required other than washing the surface with warm water and detergent to remove dirt and grease. Here, blue acrylic paint was applied to this plastic container as a background which was then covered with three coats of clear acrylic spray to protect the finished design.

Illus. 63. Wallpaper and gift-wrap paper decorate a small chest of drawers. (See page 11.)

Illus. 64. Select a plain, un-varnished breadboard, and fill any holes or defects in the wooden surface with gesso or wood filler.

Decoupage a Breadboard with Notepaper Cutouts

Illus. 65. Sand the board, and then brush on two coats of shellac to seal the wood.

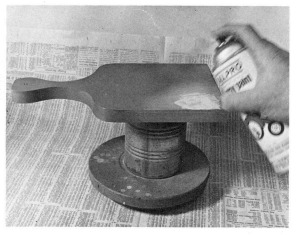

Illus. 66. When the shellac is dry, paint the board with spray enamel.

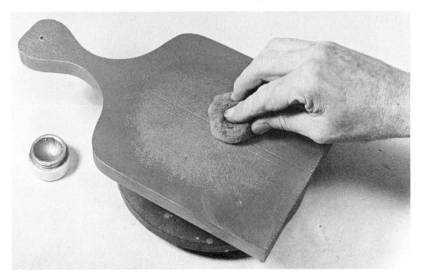

Illus. 67. Sponge paste gold in the middle of the board and rub the gold with your fingers solidly on the edges.

Illus. 68. Cut out a design from notepaper, and paste it on the breadboard.

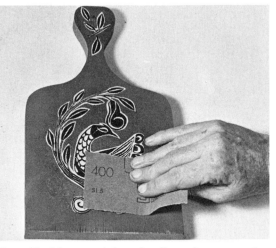

Illus. 69. After applying the first six coats of a glossy varnish, sand the board with #400 wet or dry sandpaper dipped in water. Then continue with the traditional varnishing process (page 23). See the finished breadboard in color in Illus. 60.

Illus. 70. This decoupage "painting" is composed of cutouts from reproductions from an art magazine.

Illus. 71. This wooden box, painted white and "antiqued" owes its elegance to a decoration of decoupaged metallic gold paper braid, and notepaper cutouts. (See page 34.)

Illus. 72. Gold leaf is the background for the hand-made papers and the stained-glass reproduction that decorate this elegant table top. (See page 42.)

Illus. 73. The memory of a happy vacation is preserved in this tray of hand-colored papers, metallic gold braid and photos from a travel brochure. (See page 41.)

Illus. 74. After you have sanded and sealed the wooden box, spray-paint it. White paint is being used here.

Illus. 75. Rub a brown antiquing stain over the painted surface and wipe some off until you achieve the desired effect. For best results, keep the stain light. Your decoupage design does not need competition!

Decoupage a Box with Gold Paper Braid

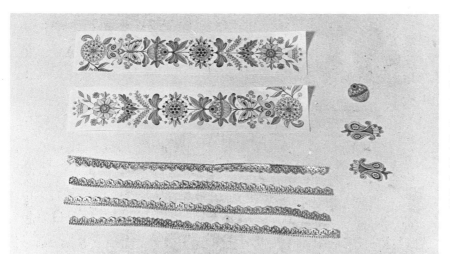

Illus. 76. Two cut-out strips of notepaper, four pieces of gold metallic paper braid (available at hobby shops) and several small motifs from notepaper have been sealed with clear acrylic spray and are ready to be pasted on the box.

Illus. 77. The two strips of notepaper, bordered by the gold braid, are pasted in a wrap-round fashion over the top and sides. The small motifs decorate the front of the box. After pasting, separate the design with a razor blade at the joining edges of the lid and box.

For this project, you will use a brown antiquing stain. Many other antiquing stains of various colors are made expressly for use in decoupage, to be applied to a painted surface and then wiped off to the desired effect. Check with your art supply and hobby shops for the one best suited to your purposes.

Illus. 78. When your design is finished, varnish and sand the box. After applying a final two coats of a satin varnish, steel-wool the box.

Illus. 79. As a final finish, apply a decoupage finishing wax to the box, and polish. See the finished box in color in Illus. 71.

Illus. 80. A stunning table is created with hand-painted, marbelized papers, plus metallic gold paper and cutouts from a tapestry book. (See next page.)

Illus. 81. This attractive plate is enhanced by decoupaged gift-wrap-paper cutouts.

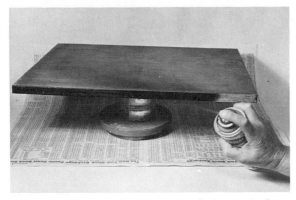

Illus. 82. Sand and seal a piece of plywood after filling in any holes or defects with gesso or wood filler. Paint the edges with a color. (Black is being sprayed on here.)

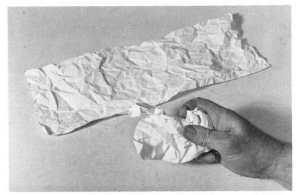

Illus. 83. Cut two strips of white paper (drawing paper, charcoal paper, and so on) to fit across each end of the plywood. Then crumple up the papers.

"Marble-Top" a Table

This is the stunning table shown on the opposite page in color (Illus. 80).

Illus. 84. Open the papers out, and wet them first with a sponge or brush. Then brush on a wash of black acrylic paint and water. The black wash will sink into the creases and produce a marbelized effect.

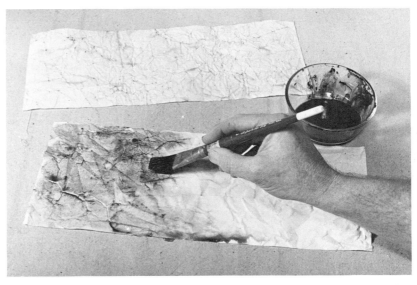

Illus. 85. Let dry and paste the marbelized papers on each end of the plywood. Flatten out with your roller over wax paper.

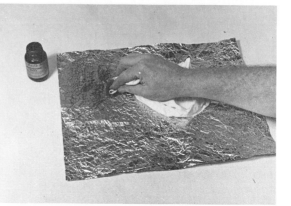

Illus. 86. Cut a piece of metallic gold paper for the middle. Measure it to overlap the marbelized papers by at least $\frac{1}{4}$ inch. Crumple the gold paper and rub a brown antiquing stain over the surface.

Illus. 87. With a ruler or T square, draw guide-lines on the marbelized paper for placement of the gold paper.

Illus. 88. Cutouts from a book of tapestry and rug designs (any patterned papers can be used) and black (acrylic) painted papers are ready to be pasted down.

Illus. 89. Following the guide-lines, paste the gold paper in place.

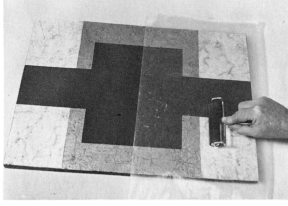

Illus. 90. Then paste the black papers down on the top to form the basic design.

Illus. 91. Add the printed cutouts to complete the design and varnish and sand in the usual manner.

Illus. 92. For a very soft, fine finish, instead of steel-wooling after the final two coats of satin varnish, sprinkle pumice powder over the table top.

Illus. 93. Then soak a rag in linseed oil, and with it, rub pumice powder over the surface in a circular motion. Clean the surface with turpentine. Then wax it with a decoupage finishing wax. Your table top will glow with the sheen of a fine piece of furniture. Hobby shops offer a variety of table legs that can be screwed to the top.

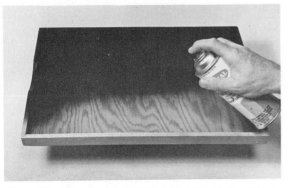

Illus. 94. Choose a raw wood tray for this project. After you have sanded and sealed the wooden tray, spray it with a flat enamel in a color that will complement your cutouts. This tray is being sprayed black.

Decoupage a Wooden Tray

Illus. 95. First, paste down a paper in a contrasting color (red acrylic paint was used here to color the paper). Then paste a strip and two circles of marbelized paper (see page 37) over the colored paper in the positions shown.

This handsome tray is being decoupaged with hand-painted papers and travel brochures. See the finished tray in color in Illus. 73.

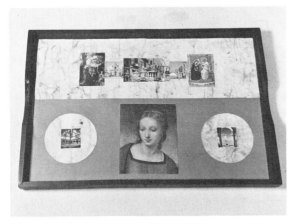

Illus. 96. Here, cutouts from Italian travel brochures are pasted down. Use your judgment as to how to place your own cutouts in effective spots.

Illus. 97. Add gold metallic paper braid to separate the areas of the design. When the design is complete, rub the edges of the tray with paste gold and varnish in the traditional way.

Gold-Leaf and Decoupage a Table Top

Gold leaf is one of the most beautiful backgrounds for decoupage. For gold leafing, you will need red paint, gold size (sizing) or varnish as an adhesive, cotton balls, or gauze pads and a book of gold leaf. For most decorating purposes, imitation gold leaf is preferable, as it is less expensive and easier to handle than real gold leaf. Imitation gold leaf comes in $5\frac{1}{2} \times 5\frac{1}{2}$-inch leaves, 25 to a book, and is available at art, hardware and hobby suppliers. Gold size is also available at these sources.

Begin your table top by sanding a piece of plywood and applying two or three coats of red

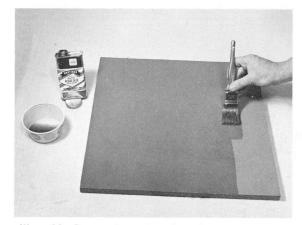

Illus. 99. Cover the painted surface with a thin coat of gold size, using a soft brush. (Varnish can also be used as an adhesive.)

Illus. 98. Sand a piece of plywood and apply two or three coats of red paint.

paint (Illus. 98). Always use red (any shade) as a base coat for gold leaf because it gives a warm glow to the gold. Acrylic paint was used in this project so that sealing of the raw wood was not necessary.

With a soft brush, cover the painted surface with a thin coat of gold size (Illus. 99). Allow the gold size to become tacky. Test the tackiness by laying your knuckle against the surface (Illus. 100). Do not use your fingers because they will leave a residue of oil on the surface. When you feel a slight pull and hear a soft snap as you pull away, the size is ready.

The quick-drying gold size that was used here took about an hour and a half to become tacky. A slow-drying gold size may take anywhere from four to eight hours. You will have to experiment with your own size. Avoid, however, a too-quick-

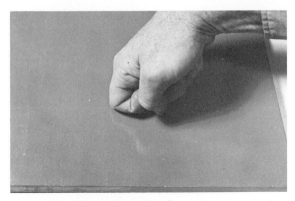

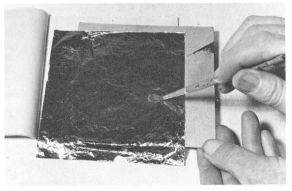

Illus. 100. Allow the gold size to become tacky. Test the tackiness by touching your knuckle against the surface.

Illus. 101. With the aid of a small brush, slide a piece of cardboard under a sheet of gold leaf, leaving a little of the leaf hanging free.

drying size because it may become completely dry before you have finished applying the gold leaf, in which case the leaf won't stick.

Slide a piece of cardboard under a sheet of gold leaf, leaving a little of the leaf hanging free.

Try not to touch the gold leaf with your fingers. Use a small brush to ease the leaf onto the cardboard (Illus. 101). Place the overhanging edges of the gold leaf on the gold size and slowly slide the cardboard out from under (Illus. 102). Lay the

Illus. 102. Carefully place the overhanging edges of the gold leaf on the edges of the gold size and slowly slide the cardboard out from under.

Illus. 103. Lay the second gold leaf in the same manner, overlapping the first by about ¼ inch.

leaf as flat as possible, but don't be disturbed by wrinkles. They will smooth out later. Also, any holes or tears can be patched up, so don't worry about them now.

Illus. 104. Continue laying the gold leaf until the entire surface is covered.

Try not to cough, sneeze or breathe heavily around gold leaf. It is very delicate and tends to go to pieces easily.

Now, lay the next sheet of gold leaf in the same way, overlapping the first by about ¼ inch (Illus. 103). You will remove this excess gold later. Continue in this manner until you have covered the entire surface (Illus. 104).

Pick up scraps of gold with a small brush and place them on any uncovered areas (Illus. 105). Don't be discouraged at the number of bare spots you may discover on your first try. Just patch them with the scraps. Actually, very small cracks or breaks where the red shows through will, more often than not, enhance the beauty of the table top.

With a ball of cotton or a folded gauze pad, tamp the gold leaf firmly into the size. When you are sure it is all down, burnish the surface by

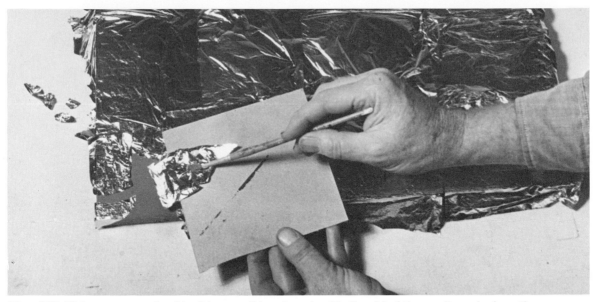

Illus. 105. Pick up scraps of gold with a small brush and, with the aid of the cardboard, place them on any uncovered areas.

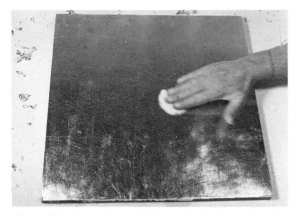

Illus. 106. Tamp the gold leaf firmly into the size with a ball of cotton. Then burnish the surface smooth with another cotton ball.

Illus. 107. Brush off all scraps of gold, let dry for 24 hours, and then spray the surface with clear acrylic spray to prevent tarnishing.

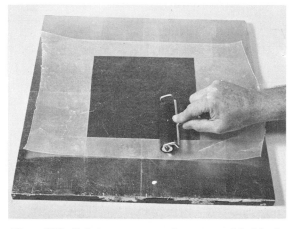

Illus. 108. Paint a square of paper with black acrylic paint and paste it in the middle of the table top.

Illus. 109. Paint another square with yellow and paste it on top of the black square, but in a diamond fashion. Inside the yellow diamond, paste a smaller red diamond.

polishing briskly with a cotton ball (Illus. 106) until it is smooth. Then brush off all scraps of gold and check again for any uncovered spots. Let the gold leaf dry for 24 hours, and then spray the surface with clear acrylic spray to prevent tarnishing, that is, if you have used imitation gold

leaf (Illus. 107). Real gold leaf, of course, will not tarnish!

Now, you are ready to decoupage your table top.

After varnishing, sanding and waxing your design, you will have a unique and stunning table

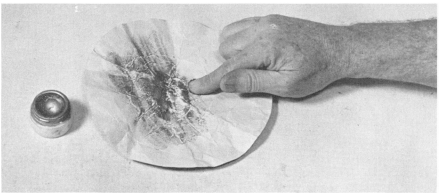

Illus. 110. Cut a circle of yellow paper. Size it to fit inside the yellow diamond. Crumple the circle and rub it with paste gold.

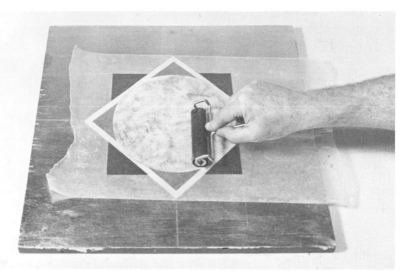

Illus. 111. Paste the gold-stained circle inside the yellow diamond.

top guaranteed to stop or start a conversation. The colors and patterns shown here are provided only as helpful hints to show you how easily you can create an effective design with just a few pieces of paper. See the finished table in color Illus. 72.

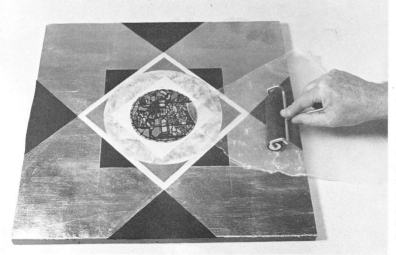

Illus. 112. Paste a small yellow square, diamond fashion, inside the circle and paste a round, printed cutout in the middle. The round magazine cutout used here is part of a stained-glass reproduction. Complete the design by cutting two black squares of paper in half, diagonally, and pasting the four pieces at the points of the yellow diamond.

Index